Old Bones and Cherry Blossoms

Selected Poems from Unprecedented Times

Diane P. Coffey

DEVOTION TO

Express the Wounds

Heal the Grief

Rest in Freedom and Wholeness

CONTENTS

INTRODUCTION

At the cusp of change, my pen rests on the desk. I have entered liminal space: The silence between the longest night of the year 2022 and the return to the growing light. Poised at the edge of completion and the unknown next step offers time to rest and reflect.

I am reminded that completion is important. Completion connotes a sense of accomplishment, closure, and preparation for the future. I hesitate to say this collection of poetry is complete; rather something more akin to a bushel of harvest gatherings prepared to be shared.

The words and images in *Old Bones* and *Cherry Blossoms* pay homage to the *unprecedented events* from the onset of the SARS COVID-19 virus into the cultural variants that mutate into global chaos and disruption. Poetic language and images captured during the *Great COVID Pause* take a penetrating look into separation, the breakdown of self-identity, and the collective breakthrough of grief, exhaustion, and fear.

Where do we go when there are no family gatherings to attend, no commute to the office, no retreats to a foreign place? How do our hearts virtually connect on a Zoom platform to mourn the unexpected losses of loved ones?

We are all connected: the people, the animals, the trees, the mountains, the stones – the earth. This collection of poems, crafted in isolation, seeks not confirmation; rather a gentle opening towards

Yes....AND

An invitation to unplug the head, take off the mask, and remember: healing is not a destination. To suffer loss and grief are part of the human experience. We need to talk about the fear we hide, the cruel reactions of anger, and the grief that we may never get over.

Old Bones and *Cherry Blossoms* is my broadband sweep and my intimate dive beneath medical health statistics, hardwired technology and media platforms into the innate wisdom that resides within each of us. My gift to share is for us, alone and together, to look into the mirror, to be touched by words, and to feel into this healing balm offering through the simple organic nature of poetry.

Read the collection from cover to cover or randomly select pages. The choice is yours. Pick and choose what resonates and return as often as you wish and then, let it all dissolve into new beginnings:

Stand in the shadow feeling into brokenness.

Remember through our rootedness that we are all connected.

Shift your perspective and let go of what no longer supports your wellbeing and the wellbeing of our planet.

Continually commit to living your wholeness.

Influenced by a global community, this poetess is deeply grateful for the dynamic gifts of the mystical teachers and movement artists seeded in this collection. Essential to healing into wholeness, be it past time, now time, or waiting on the horizon, *Old Bones* and *Cherry Blossoms* is an offering of fierce compassion for tumultuous times.

PART I

INVOCATION

Heartfelt Centering

We call

All the blood lines

Vessels of body

Earth inlets

Deciduous and Coniferous Trees

Old Oak and Cherry Blossoms

Oceans and rivers

Mountain peaks and canyons wide

Ancestors

Animal Allies

Spirit and Soul

All who share the love

Of imagination

Mystical and magical

The alchemical process

Mixing word and image

Meditation…Movement…Matrix

PART II

BREAK DOWN

BREAK OPEN

BREAK THROUGH

Initiation

Emotions erupt

Remnants of grief

Scatter

Beneath falling water

    River rapid

    Churns inside

    Confusion twisted in undertow

    Tumbles over rugged rocks

Tossed across an empty beach

10,000 grains of sand

No measure for internal turmoil

    One strike

    Clenched fist to chest

    One heart beat

    A gasp for air

Listen

Systolic heart beat

Stillness

Alive in the breath

Alive in the Pause

The nib moves

Fine lines

Midnight colored ink

Flows in cursive shapes

        Words matter

        Prose

        Cross borders

Penned in solitude

Inside Zoom rooms

Pass from cell to cell

        Written in lockdown

        Organized text

        Numbered pages

        Connections delivered

        Embodied in the vibration

        Energized from the heart center

        Enlivened in the pause

.

Nobody Knows My Sorrow

Global Pandemic
Waiting to exhale
Long Covid prevails
Unemployment doom
Home evictions
Scarcity
Who matters?
BPOC
LGBTQ
Everybody's got troubles
#Me Too
We're all tired
Run to catch a train, plane
Hop a bus
Catch a freeway green light
Distractions
Check email
Post to Instagram
Friend a request on Facebook
Emoji Text reply

Mass shootings
Politicians contradict and divide
Cheat, lie, steal
Truth resides in the unknown
Wild fires rage
Volcanos erupt
Tornado winds
Hurricane destruction
Tsunami waves
Landscape of doom, gloom and destruction

Prick of the Needle

Well behaved
Perfect in character
Like Godiva chocolate
Secret center preserved in gold foil

Finely tuned
Stradivarius
Harmonious immune system

Until the global COVID-19 spell was cast

Against deeper wisdom
Poison injected
For no other reason than to protect others

Needle prick left arm
Second vaccine dose
Reacts

Like a fairy tale
She falls into a deep sleep
What ails you dear one?

On the surface too much heat
Homeostasis in chaos
Hot lava bubbles below the skin

Tectonic plates
Converge in sulfuric fire and ash
Fever and sweat purge toxins
What remedy is needed?
Lion's alchemical roar
Salt water tears sting
Remember like cures like

Wounded Healer

Corridors converge at right angles
Perpendicular hallways intersect
Hydraulic lift doors glide open
Emergency Room doors slide shut
Hallways merge in a geographical maze

"Wait, I'm lost"
Acoustical tiles reverberate
"Late – can't wait"
"Please wait!"

Dear ER Team
Please allow me to introduce
My Body
The most sophisticated healing machine you will ever meet
Together, we work as a team
Please honor my body's innate wisdom
Please respect my individuality
Not all bodies respond the same
Some parts are generic,
Others unique

Let there be no doubt
I am the authentic model
Sensitive
Intuitive
Bright

Not your typical allopathic textbook study
Please ask probing questions
Pay attention to the responses
Listen to the body's innate wisdom

Destined to break the rules

Experiment with color

Shape

Texture

Mix and match

Compare and contrast

Not one or the other

Both

Neither

Shard #1 The Essential ME

Kryptonite

Blindly feel
Suffer the dis-ease
Silently mourn
Call me stubborn
Accuse me of denial

Maybe
Just maybe
I'm scared beyond words
Touch the incision
Branded wound
Bear the markings of grief

    Irregular architecture
    Invasive carcinoma
        Replay
            But that's a story for another day

COVID-19 virus variants
Kryptonite

Choiceless events
What are we initiating into?

Lean back
Breathe into the void
See what you see
Hear what you hear
Learn what you learn

Presence with feet on the earth
Resilience resides here
The unpaved road will be the guide

Love Letter to My Sister

Miss you
Miss you every day, dear *Sisto*
Miss the conversations only sisters share

Long for the stories shared between siblings
Our giggles and our tears
I love you like only a sister can

The love and kindness you have for family is heart opening
The sound of your voice when you sweetly say his name – *Dylan*
The tenderness of a *Grammy* filled with love

Your immense love for *your daughters* is steadfast
You teach core values and model strong work ethics
You mirror the unconditional love of our *Nana* as a gift to your children,
and, your children's children

I admire your dedication to your marriage
You nurture and love
Like no other
You give selflessly to ensure the finest care

It's no accident that I am married to an Aries
The archetypal characteristics my *Sisto* shares with my husband
Loyal and faithful
Helpful and tolerant
Heaven knows I need them

There are no mistakes
We came into this world to share this path
To grow
To evolve
And to dissolve into nothing less than pure LOVE

Sisterly love
Love of family

The Witness

"Don't try to cover your tears with a smile. Look at everything you've been through to get HERE."

Said the Witness.

There's no place to hide the despair
The shame and guilt
The sorrow and suffering

Broken down
Broken open

Tears fall into the arms of compassion
Into the embrace of kindness
Held within the heart
Where the pulse of love circulates
In and through you

You are not alone
You are not invisible

I see you

I love you

Night Journey

Silence rests on muted words

Divested of cover
Naked to the bone
Body held in deep contraction

Daughter of the night
Unforgiving witness
Dreaded memories

What would rather be forgotten?

The body knows

In the darkness of despair
Seen with double insight
What's yours
and
Not mine

What's not mine?
Anger
Betrayal
Deceit

My authentic truth
        Sees imaginal possibilities
Dreams with fierce compassion
        and
Loving kindness

Hold fast to gooey
Chocolate *S'mores*

Dance naked under the stars

Sing along with Cole Porter

"Oh, give me land,
Lots of land under starry skies above.
Don't fence me in.
Let me ride through the wide open
Country that I love."

Shard #2 The Essential ME

My Country 'tis of Thee

Where are the doors that open wide?
The welcome greeting
Our connection exchanged in a heartfelt embrace
Bear hugs
Body hugs
Arms extend wide
Wrap around
Memories of feeling human touch
Voices from long ago
Remember the rock star lyrics

Feel me
Touch me
Heal me

Remember "America"

My country 'tis of thee
Land of sweet liberty

Where are you now?

Put down your rapid-fire arms
Surrender violence
Anger and rage

Remember

Hold shattered hearts with tenderness
Listen to uncontrollable sobs of sorrow
Fierce compassion

Feel our collective pain and mourn

PART III

THE STORIES THAT MATTER

Maui Messenger

The story begins at the edge of an island jungle in the middle of the ocean far from my hone land. My thoughts are embedded in fear.

How am I going to hold change? Like an addict I see myself slipping back into old patterns and everything new is lost.

Sad, disappointed, and feeling alone I leave my room to walk to the nearby market for something to eat. As I walk with purpose a man in a broken-down wheel chair crosses my path and asks if I can push him to IHOP?

The old patterns of thoughts race through my head:

> Will he rob me?
>
> Will he beat me?
>
> Will he rape me?
>
> Will he kill me?

I reply: "Ok - I think I know where IHOP is."

I try to push the wheel chair, but it does not move.

He says: "You have to pull me; my chair is broken!"

The man has a strong body odor, wears tattered clothes, and I guess must weigh at least 200-pounds. Walking backwards with this heavy load is hard for me. I cannot see where I am going as I weave backwards. It's impossible to navigate a straight path.

My breathing is labored. I remember I have not taken my daily asthma medication.

We arrive at a construction area where the path narrows.

Again, the old patterns of fear:

> Will he rape me?
>
> Rob me?
>
> Beat me?
>
> Kill me?

Midway through the construction area one of the wheel chair's wheels collapses. The chair will not move.

He says: "Now you can push the chair."

Pushing the wheel chair forward, it picks up momentum until we reach the end of the construction area.

I don't see the IHOP signage. I panic thinking I have gone the wrong way and now we're lost.

Continuing to the end of the sidewalk I turn my head to the right and see the IHOP sign: Our destination insight!

I ask if he wants to go inside IHOP, or wait outside?

He says: YES! He wants to go in.

I look at the entrance and ponder: How am I going to navigate the chair through the doorway?

Two adults stand behind us chatting and paying no attention to my dilemma.

Suddenly a little girl swings the door and says: "I'll hold the door for you!"

I survey the threshold. How am I going to get enough momentum to get the wheel chair safely over the threshold riser?

As if reading my mind, the wheel chair bound man places his hands on either side of the doorway and pulls himself and the chair over the threshold and through the doorway.

Quietly He says "Thank you, I know this was hard on you."

Yes!   The message I needed to hear!

The acknowledgement delivered by an unexpected messenger.

> Remember the kindness of a child
>
> Open your heart to another
>
> Walk away free from the shackles of the past
>
> You are enough
>
> Your service to others matters

Yes, you will find ways to navigate change – one step at a time.

7 X 7

This tale may be hard for some to read. The language might be offensive and the gallows humor a bit too graphic, but it is the raw truth.

The story begins as I arrive in San Francisco. This is a layover stop before departing from the Golden State of California destined for the east coast. At the height of my career, I lived in San Francisco and am intimately familiar with the various neighborhoods. But on this visit, I see the city through a different lens.

To my dismay the City's downtown streets are littered with shocking scenes, one after another. Many of the street medians are lined with tents and make shift dwellings. Disoriented naked people dodge cars in the street, whilst others sleep on sidewalks with their arms spread out like Christ on the Cross.

San Francisco: 7 x 7 $= 49$ square miles of natural beauty and 7 deadly sins. Is this a vulnerable and at-risk subculture, or another flower power transient San Francisco phase?

The San Francisco scene becomes a flashback to the 1985 iconic film *Mad Max Thunderdome* and the town run on pig shit. *Mad Max Thunderdome* stars music icon Tina Turner as Auntie Entity and Mel Gibson as Mad Max. Wearing a mini length chain dress Auntie explains how Barter Town's electrical supply depends on a crude methane refinery powered by pig feces.

Now it's time to come clean. Before arriving in San Francisco, I spent several weeks in nature hiking mountains in search of waterfalls and skipping waves at the beach. To leave the dirt and sand behind I take my laundry to a public laundromat. As I walk through the laundromat, I see many of the washing machines are inoperable. The coin boxes have been removed with the exception of a few at the rear of the building. Apparently, the fear of theft is greater than operating a fully functional business.

As I walk down the aisle of washing machines, I see a woman dressed in a patched pink housecoat and canvas shoes with no laces. She is squatting on the floor defecating in a plastic bag. I avert my eyes and walk away in an attempt to give her some privacy.

Like the washing machines the coin boxes have been removed from the soap dispenser and there's no soap available to purchase. Even if you have money, you can't buy soap in this laundromat.

Two adults with two children walk into the laundromat with baskets of clothes to wash. I ask if I can buy a pod of soap. The man asks how many I need? Not wanting to be greedy and ask for more than I need, I reply, "only one, maybe two pods." He counts his pods of soap and hands me one saying: "You don't need to pay me, just pay it forward."

Gracious generosity from one who barely has enough to meet their own needs.

There's a patisserie across the street where I can buy a muffin to give to the woman in the pink housecoat.

As I cross the street, I notice the woman's plastic bag of shit has been placed outside the laundromat at the curb.

Is this a thoughtful act to avoid smelling up the entire laundromat? How often are the laundromat trash cans emptied!

Or, is the woman making a statement for everyone to look at living life on the street?

I think about how often I've watched dog walkers scoop dog poop into scented biodegradable bags that can be tossed into city trash containers. There are City Ordinances and Fines to be paid for failure to pick up after your dog.

I return from the patisserie to find the woman standing at the clothes folding table reading a newspaper. I place the bag with the muffin on the folding table. She quickly pushes the bag away and with righteous wrath in her voice:

"I don't eat sweets!"

I walk away envying her discipline to eat healthy.

I then watch the woman turn to filling a plastic Tide detergent bottle with water from the laundromat utility sink. She takes the plastic Tide bottle outside. A few minutes later she returns and repeats the sequence of filling the bottle and going outside. Her ritual repeats for about six trips outside.

In my imagination I think maybe she is bathing her body outside on the streets for everyone to watch.

From the trail of water on the sidewalk, I can see she is watering the trees on California Street, and not bathing her own body as I had speculated.

Three generations of my family were farmers. I grew up surrounded by decomposing matter. The microbiome being critical to the environmental, human and animal life cycle. There is no slothfulness about the lone woman as she waters the trees and serves the natural environment in this metropolitan community.

San Francisco fecal matter has brought me up close and personal to life on the streets, as well as a vocabulary stretch: shit, feces, crap, poop, dung, excrement, fecal matter, defecation, bullshit, waste, manure, stool, bowel movement, body waste, sewage, and then there are the countless terms children make up spontaneously that could add another dimension to my list.

Before leaving San Francisco, I am invited to the Pacific Heights home of an old friend for dinner. The front door mat greets me:

As I tell my laundry story, my host is shocked at my use of a public laundromat. He can't understand why I did not bring my soiled laundry to his home to be washed. I try to explain the nature of beach sand and how it leaves a trail but I am met with more disgust.

My friend serves a feast of a meal, more than his dinner guest can eat. The leftover food is packed up and driven to a central location where street dwellers are known to congregate. As the food is offered someone calls out:

"Did you bring wine to go with the food?"

Surely, I'll be on someone's shit list for starting the conversation at the end of the digestive process rather than COVID-immunity, variants, or the top of the socio-economic dung.

Gluttony is no different from the peak of Pacific Heights down to the flat lands of the Tenderloin District: The lust for caviar offered seven ways with a beverage of choice: Sauvignon Blanc or Bordeaux.

I re-tell this story with dis-ease. As pandemics spread globally what new and variant bacterial infections are being unleashed on the streets? What is happening to the human condition?

Living values are grounded deep within my soul:

Nourishment matters
Kindness and generosity matter
Pay it forward matters
Tending trees and the environment matters
Our care for one another matters

Remember

We may never know names
Share contact information

But we will recognize
Body movements
The sway of limbs

We will remember
Pulse
Vibrations
Heart Beats
Frequencies of the unspoken words

PART IV

TREE WHISPERER

Rooted

Deeply rooted in the cycle of nature

The wheel of the year

Precious moments

Within the continuum of time

Always moving within

The harmony and the chaos

Tend and gestate

Renew

Recreate

Chameleons

Astride our pink blankets
We ride the brisk air
Across the blue sky
We escape the mundane

Once upon a time
Illusionists soar through time
Roam wide-open space with boundless freedom

Chameleons cast spells of invisibility
Exquisitely spun threads of finely shorn memories
Our pink blankets
Magic cloaks with alchemical properties

Over the river and through the woods
Up the hill and around the bend
Remember to wave as we pass Grandmother's house

Together we weave tales
Journey into the great unknown
We are the shape shifting generation

8:46 a.m.

"I can't breathe"

On May 25, 2020 George Floyd, a 46-year-old black American man was killed in Minneapolis, Minnesota during an arrest for allegedly using a fake $20 bill to purchase cigarettes at a grocery store.

Repeatedly world viewers watched the media replay of Mr. Floyd's arrest, restraint, and final words: "I can't breathe."

My chest contracts, I hold my breath, praying silently for someone to say "STOP! holding that man down."

Now, it's too late.

Into the forest I go to find presence with the trees…

In the Presence of Trees

Our feet touch the earth
The place where we all connect
Trees, flowers, roaming bears
Touched by events
Presence
No protection
Marching feet on city streets
Moved by loss of life
The land grieves with deep sorrow
Presence
Witness hurt and pain
In places where trees are few and far between
And people cannot breathe
The intelligence of trees
Witness the every day
Pain and sorrow
Anger and grief
Trees know
Presence
Deeply rooted in a past
Burrowed in cement cracks
Suffocated by lack of light
Pleas and begging cries silenced
Night begets darkness
Gentle giants stand in solidarity
Mark hollow grounds like tombstones
While rage is set ablaze
Presence
Witness the every day
Trees know
Pain and sorrow … anger and grief
Deep roots and strong prayers
Stand at the threshold of the future
Presence knows wholeness

Tree Seers Invocation

We are the Tree Seers
Lone Oak and Forest Evergreen

Connected to all
Deeply rooted
We tap and spread
Away from and into Mother Earth

Present in now time
Past time
Time future

Trunks and crown branches stretch
Skyward
Limbs for winged ones to perch
Rest their nests
Leaves bud and fall

Changing seasons
Cycles of life and death
In stillness and raging storms
Bough and bend
Char in fire's flame

Renew with rain life force
Seeds scatter
Carried on the winds
Borough deep into the earth

Tree Whisperers
Bough and bend
In gratitude
Listen
This is Tree Seer Wisdom

Pantomime of Solitude

Tree of life
Weeping Willow
Deeply rooted

Leaf covered branches
Changing flora fauna
Woodpeckers drum
In staccato exuberance

Silence
Pantomime of solitude
Without dialogue
Sans gesture

Spark of the divine within
Mirrored in wild unprotected places
Planted in my soul

Old bones rest upon earth's fertile womb

Wild Edge

the vistas expand across the horizon
beyond what the eye can see
this is the place

the *Wild Edge*
where feet stomp
cells expand and contract
breath moves in and out
heart beats in rhythm
connect you to me
and me to you

driven to the edge by chaos
we meet betwixt and between
solid earth meets flowing tides of change
at the threshold to greater self

the *Wild Edge*
fearless here and there
past and future
we meet at the *Wild Edge*

the *Wild Edge*
calls to the untamed and passionate
hidden treasures within each of us

fragrant smells of night blooming jasmine
infused in the sweet taste of ambrosia
hidden treasures
waiting to be discovered
at the *Wild Edge*

Valley of My Soul

I came to this valley
Wanderer on a path
Taking the right turn at the fork in the road
Follow the steep incline
And at the mountain ridge
Begin the deep descent

I came into this valley
Passing the fire charred terrain
The ash covered soil
The smokey frankincense smells
Imbued endings

I came to this valley
To roam the mountain range
And drop into rolling hills
Burrow my body deep in fresh green clover
To remember my inner landscape

I came to this valley
To cross the mountain pass
Stand with the charred trees
To ask permission to return
To be renewed by mountain dew

I came into the valley of my soul
To open my heart
To reimagine the seasons of my life
In a new story

I came here
At this moment in time
To witness the buds of new beginnings

Blossom into possibilities

All That is Precious Turns Within

Oh, precious oak tree
Anchored in decomposing humus
Weathered bark of twisted knots
Mark growth and age
Branches embrace the wind
Dance with multicolored leaves
Wild birds gather
Their songs a twill of melodies

Grass woven nest hidden on outstretched limbs
Changing season impregnate new life
All that's precious turns from within
Seeds germinate
Bloom
Acorns fall to the earth
Bestow abundant harvest

Time frozen in stillness
Listen to the quiet
There are voices to be heard within the silence
A call to rise up

Push forth new buds from fertile ground
Rise up
Once more my precious
So that I might rest beneath your outstretched limbs
Lay me down

Upon rich, dark, decomposed organic humus

PART V

KALEIDOSCOPE

Hey!

Wake Up!

The t ime is now

Wake Up!

Time to tell a new story

Kaleidoscope

Shards of language

Broken phrases

Shift back and forth

Mirror play

Angles and patterns in motion

        Fragments of poetry

        Shift perspectives

Words written on pages

Movement in motion

           Spoken words rolling across tongue

           Landing in the pause

           Between heartbeats – yours and mine

Each beat with intention

        Or not

        Entwine together

        Twist and turn

        See through

        Form new lens

Too Much

Fear knocks at the door
Dressed in dark
Coco brown cashmere overcoat
Beneath shadowed brow
Eyes penetrate
Hold captive
Blue jays squawk
We're all exhausted
Grieving
Scared

Too much energy invested in fear
Time wasted on misdeeds
Missing trust – mistrust
River birch whispers
It's not too late

Time has not run out
Sip the healing elixir of surrender
Offer heartfelt compassion
Share forgiveness with yourself and others

Trust comes at the edge
Stripped down
Naked

Wholeness welcomes fear
Rise from the darkness
Sit beneath the lunar eclipse
Seeds of change gather
Revealed in the internal landscape

Muse blues

I got you Babe

Under my Skin

Shard #3 The Essential ME

Veinti Veinti

Lean back

Witness with 2020 vision

Feel images in shapes
textures
and color

See gray
between black and white

Lean back
Listen
Hear language
Aliterate sounds
Metaphoric meanings

Keep it real
Truth camouflaged
In the convex
Concave
Lens of half truths

What do you see?

Tide Song

Waiting for an ocean tide song
A wave of ebb and flow song

Listen
For an ocean tide song
Rhythmic breath moves like shifting tides
At surf's edge

Waiting for an ocean tide song
A life-giving song

Receive breath
A wave of ebb and flow song

With Siren's allure
Dancing on the rocks
Diving beneath the surf

Waiting for an ocean tide song

Do you hear the unspoken words?

Ports of Call

Time to pull up anchor
Push off from shore

Drift silently with the tide
Flow with the current

Remember when we first met
Recall the many ports of call

From here to there
Then and now

Love carried
From distant shores
Through rough waters
To caverns deep

Infinite waves of love
From the edge of this reality
To reaches beyond all time

Infinite love
Always present
Reflected in each passing wave

Afterglow

Water lilies capture the timeless ripple of river's flow

Aesthetic beauty

Mystery revealed

Dance with the strength of the earth
Merge with compassionate knowing.

Voice raised on radical winds
Sweep away righteousness

Natural harmony
Destined to rekindle an old flame

Reflection

Fondle the afterglow

PART VI

HEALING IS NOT A DESTINATION

Remember the sky you were born under and each of the star stories? *Canis Majoris*, Sirius, the dog star is the brightest star in the night sky. My totem, my family core value, is made visible in the image of the canine / human totem symbolizing a natural relationship to family and community. The origin of the word totem means *mark of my family*. In nature a dog pack functions like a family and carries a similar social structure.

Safety and security are felt when dogs are part of a family and have established roles. Developing a relationship with a four legged one requires listening carefully, paying attention and tuning into their expressions. Dogs communicate somatically, through body language and nonverbal communications.

Tending the needs of these beloved creatures - their physical, emotional, psychological, spiritual, intellectual and surrounding environment gives shape and rhythm to my life. The instinctual reality of the animal world grounds me in ways unlike other work.

I travel daily in the company of dogs. With each twist and turn along the path I try to stay open to the places they take me and to the sights and sounds I might have missed were it not for them.

Nose to the ground, I follow the smells, listen for the distant howls and struggle for fluency in their native language. Subtle shifts in ears, tails and other body parts tell a story

Dogs are noble animals. Their loyalty may supersede how humans treat them. Dogs tend to have a compassionate understanding of human shortcomings.

Of all the gifts dogs offer perhaps the greatest is the opportunity to delve deep inside ourselves without judgment or timetables, with patience, and their amazing capacity for forgiveness.

Compass Point

What are you looking for?

A place to land

Presence in the movement

Lost treasures

Remembered

Simple

Slow

Small

Step

Into the Unknown

Center Stage

On beat
Off rhythm
In time
No time

Gold between these toes
Silence beneath
Stillness

Tread gently on fresh ground
Tilled with inspiration and insight
Sink down into rich, dark, decay

Stand center stage
Listen
Alone and together

Who am I?

Am I too literal?
Too dreamy?

Too much?
Not enough?

Map of my soul
Soles of my feet
Rise with the moon

Long to be taken

Out of head

into body

To dance in ecstasy

Shard #4 The Essential ME

Metamorphosis

Poised betwixt and between
Colorful bodies in motion
Arrive to tell another story

Night travelers and soul seekers
Soar with feet on the ground
Profound vessels of transformation
Free falling to places never planned

Beautiful bodies dance in ecstasies
Full bodied terrain
Portraits of plentitude
Thoughts embrace silence

Poetry and movement
The alchemical experience
Spoken words land in the pause
Tread lightly on Mother Earth
Her rhythm in tune

In tune

With all that matters

Medicine Bag

Unmasked in the dance
Rhythm and beats
Mixed in Soundcloud

Attuned souls listen
Stargazing reflections
Witness

Do tell
What's in your medicine bag?
Treasure trove of elements
Feather headpiece
Ritual concha shell
Stones and bones
Breath of fire

The embodied operating system
Vibrates real feelings
Feel your emotions

The energetic vibrations
Chi and Kundalini rise
Plant medicine, Chinese Herbs, Ayurvedic meals
Nourish and heal

The Laws of Similarity call in the wisdom of the body
Feel your body
The potency
The wisdom
Whole body resilience

Medicine Bag rooted in all ways
Ancient and real

Call to the Wild

Sounds of bird chatter
Call and response
The audience settles in
Prelude to
This movement
This poem
This dance

Wood winds fade
Only a trilling bird solo
To accompany this interior landscape

Hands poised
Offer gifts
One step
The beginning movement
Step to the side

Red cardinals whisper
Gentle nudge
Pay attention
Spin round
Step back
Slowly
Circle around this body

Listen
Wings flutter
Touch ever so light
Sends chills through the body
Hands poised in offering
Into the interior of the cave
Where SHE/HE/THEY awaits with open heart

Cadence

Eccentric beyond wild dreams
Raw
Untamed

Natural rhythm
Poetry like dance
Speechless

Unable to take the next step
The words don't come
Primitive sounds

Drums
Wood reeds
Echo call and response

Lean in close
Whisper secrets
Organic and real

What does your poem say?
Eccentric
Desire to be wild

Playful cadence

Seeks raw
Untamed
Natural rhythm

Your vibrant sensual self

Everything and Nothing

Bud
Bloom
Blossom

Beautiful
Butterfly
Brooder

Busy
Bees
Buzz

Bud
Bloom
Blossom

BE

Lineage

Heart centered generosity
Breathe in the presence of the ancestors
Sniff out the animal spirits
Rooted in nature

Curanderos – medicine women
Grandmothers illuminate
Nurture and nourish
Generations of bones and blood

This body a living link
Night Seer - Shaman
Anchored in mud and stars
Wisdom keeper

Ancestors – remind me who I am.

Farming family
Stewards of Chumash Land
Garden tillers
Tenders of fruit bearing trees

Artists
Dancing ritualists
Creatrix

Who are you today?

I am

LIGHT and SHADOW

Essential ME

I love surrealism
Dada for sure
Mix image and word

Creatrix of dancing poetry
Movement in motion

I love words written on pages
Spoken words rolling across tongue
Landing un the pause
Between heartbeats – yours and mine

Like Chinese jump rope
Enter the field
Each beat with intention
Or not
Weave tangled webs
Twist and turn

Long to be taken
Out of my head into my body
To dance in ecstasy

A wild messy artist
I love the feel
Thick girth
Scribble brush held tightly in hand
Stroke…Slide
Splash…Slither
Serenade
Muse blues
> *I got you Babe*
> *Under my Skin*

I am a curious artist
Destined to break the rules
Experiment with color
Shape…Texture
Mix and match
Compare and contrast
Not one or the other
Both?
Neither

Hold fast to chocolate gooey *S'mores*

Dance beneath the star covered sky
Raise voice in song

Sing along with Cole Porter

> "Oh, give me land,
> Lots of land under starry skies above.
> Don't fence me in.
> Let me ride through the wide open
> Country that I love."

A call to create
Meditation…Movement… Metaphor
My response
Sensual…Sentient
Still silence

---

*Note to Reader: "Teaspoon by Teaspoon"
Fragments of "The Essential ME" are intentionally scattered throughout this collection. Identified by number, the Shards are bite size pieces to ponder.

Gratitude Lights the Path

I see your loving heart
I feel the scared reality we are living in

I see you
Standing present in this moment

Not escaping to some other place
Anchored to the earth
Not sinking into invisibility

Present in your temple body
Heart filled with gratitude
Safe within your sacred body

Gratitude glows with each glance
Gratitude joins hands with grace in beauty and suffering
There's no need to make huge decisions

Gratitude lights the path with a golden light

Melt the overwhelm into trust
Teaspoon by teaspoon
Dissolve grief into love
Let go of the drama and victimhood
Set simple small sweet intentions

Embrace each day with gratitude

Gracias Madre, Gracias Padre, Gracias Abuelas

Thank you

Spirit, Guides, Angels, Teachers, Ancestors, Lovers,

Animal Allies, 4-Diections, Mother Earth / Creator

ART AND PHOTO CREDITS
ORIGINAL PHOTOGRAPHS AND ART
FOR THE PURPOSE OF THIS PUBLICATION
APPEAR IN BLACK AND WHITE

PAGE NO.

COVER "HEART BLOSSOMS"
Pen and Ink, San Francisco, California
(c) Diane P. Coffey. 2019

14 "HEART CENTERED".
Mixed Media Photograph
(c) Diane P. Coffey. 2020

18 "DAUGHTER OF THE NIGHT".
ACRYLIC PAINT
(c) Diane P. Coffey. 2020

30 "O SHIT NOT YOU AGAIN"
Door Mat
Available at Wayfair
Trinx Oh Shit-- Not You Again 30 in. x 18 in.
Outdoor Door Mat | Wayfair

34 "SEER ORACLE"
Mixed Media Mask #5
(c) Diane P. Coffey. 2022

38 "LISTENING"
Photograph Fresno, California
(c) Diane P. Coffey. Circa 1956

42 "VALLEY OF MY SOUL"
Photograph Santa Ynez Valley, California
(c) Diane P. Coffey. 2020

For the love of living in freedom and wholeness
this is what we do when waiting for change:

Proceeds for the sale of *Old Bones and Cherry Blossoms* may be donated
to one / all of the following:

The Institute for Poetic Medicine
www.poeticmedicine.org

The Painting Experience
www.processarts.com

The World Central Kitchen
World Central Kitchen (wck.org)

Hip Pocket Theatre
www.hippocket.org

The 360 Emergence
The 360 Emergence | The 360 Emergence

And many spontaneous random acts of kindness

ABOUT THE AUTHOR

Diane P. Coffey is a lifetime artist in residence – at home – crafting mixed media art, stories to tell, and blending image and language. Both dance and writing have been at the heart of her artistry since adolescence. She was raised in Central California and holds a doctorate degree in Mythological Studies and Depth Psychology from Pacifica Graduate Institute.

Diane's spoken word "*I Lumination*: An Interior Experiment Theatre" was performed live in 2019 at University of California, Santa Barbara during the Art and Psyche: Conference IV and subsequently made into a docufilm set against a backdrop of California landscape.

Diane currently lives in suburban Philadelphia with her life partner and their beloved rescue pit bull *Moo Moo Xie Xie* – her name an expression of gratitude every time spoken.

Made in the USA
Las Vegas, NV
25 January 2023

66270641R00056